this prayer journal belongs to

_____

_____

date

"I will lift up my eyes to the mountains; from where shall my help come?
My help comes from the LORD, who made heaven and earth."—*Psalm 121:1–2*

prayers *of* my heart

a personal
~ prayer journal ~

debbie williams

HOWARD
PUBLISHING CO

Our purpose at Howard Publishing is to:

- *Increase faith* in the hearts of growing Christians
- *Inspire holiness* in the lives of believers
- *Instill hope* in the hearts of struggling people everywhere

Because He's coming again!

Prayers of My Heart © 2004 by Debbie Taylor Williams
All rights reserved. Printed in the United States of America
Published by Howard Publishing Co., Inc.
3117 North 7th Street, West Monroe, LA 71291-2227
www.howardpublishing.com

06 07 08 09 10 11 12 13 14 15   12 11 10 9 8 7 6 5 4 3

Edited by Philis Boultinghouse
Interior design by Stephanie D. Walker and LinDee Loveland

ISBN 1-58229-443-7; ISBN 1-58229-558-1 (pbk.)

Scripture taken from the NEW AMERICAN STANDARD BIBLE ®, Copyright © 1960,
1962, 1963, 1968, 1971, 1972, 1973, 1975, 1977, 1995 by The Lockman Foundation. Used
by permission.

Dedication

To my husband, Keith, who prays for me and with me

To our children, Taylor and Lauren, whose very lives are answers to prayer

To my sisters, Linda McConnico and Vicki Good, whose prayers are invaluable to me

To my mother, Bernice Taylor, who taught me to pray

To Araceli Torres, whose prompting caused me to make this journal available

To Cynthia Itschner, for her hours of prayers and editing

To JoAnn Dealey, for using her gifts of design and presentation to create the original cover

To Kathleen Reeve, Linda Schmidt, and Nancy Turner, for their work on the journal

To our Lord and Savior, Jesus Christ, who intercedes for us

May each who holds intimacy with the Almighty as precious draw near to Him

…in silence and prayer,

…in devotion and discipline,

…in honesty and confession.

For the lover of your soul will not leave you or deceive,

but we must *listen* with our hearts and

learn with our eyes

what He would show us!

Welcome

Most people want to pray.

As a matter of fact, studies show that most people do pray. Prayer is a powerful blessing. It is the means by which we enter into communion with God. The Bible teaches us that God hears our prayers (Psalm 65) and responds according to His name (John 14:13–14).

All of us promise the traditional, "I'll pray for you," when needs are expressed. And we sincerely try to honor those promises of prayer, but we are often disappointed in ourselves when we neglect to pray as we should.

Several years ago in an attempt to find a concise way to record prayer requests, I developed the column-based prayer chart in this journal. It was an answer to prayer, for I had been praying for a way to keep up with the prayer needs of my spouse, children, family, friends, church, ministry, as well as the unsaved and our nation. I had struggled for years to find a way that worked well for me. I tried many methods, including other prayer journals, but my prayer lists were never organized in a way that worked well for me. Prayer columns, like the ones in this journal, finally gave me the efficient, easy-to-use method I needed.

The Benefits of Column-Based Prayer Journaling

By journaling in a column under a person's name, repeated requests need not be re-recorded. For instance, I pray for my family every day. Certain urgent and pressing requests for my family often remain the same over a period of time. The prayer columns allow me to record the request once, instead of repeating the same request over and over.

Another benefit to journaling in a column format is the ease of recording answered prayers. Rather than searching for requests in a volume of multiple names and pages, I can easily glance under a person's name, find the request that has been answered, and record God's response. Highlighting or dating God's answer to my prayer is powerful, as I see and praise God for His goodness and faithfulness in that person's life.

Three Formats in One Journal

In this journal, you will find three different sections to help you in your prayer journey. Two of them are column based, and the third allows room for longer prayers and meditations.

(Examples of how to use these three formats can be found in the appendix.)

May you be blessed as you draw near to the Lord in intimacy and prayer.

Month at a Glance

First, let's look at the "Month at a Glance" section in your prayer journal.

There are twelve pages, one page for each month of the year. As friends call with special prayer requests for surgery, an important job interview, or a test, you can turn to your "Month at a Glance" calendar and record the request. Only a few words are necessary: John—surgery, Amber—test. You may also want to record birthdays in this section, so you can pray for people on their special day.

As you look at each month, you can see at a glance what you need to pray for. It is also easy to highlight, date, or place a check mark by the request when you see God's answer.

Week at a Glance

The next section you will note in the prayer journal is the "Week at a Glance" portion. It is designed for you to write the names of those you are praying for at the top of each column. Under the column, you can record prayer requests. It is here that you will rejoice as you see God's hand moving in the lives of those for whom you pray.

Look now at the samples in the "Week at a Glance" sample in the appendix. Notice how the names of those being prayed for are recorded in the column headings across the top of the prayer chart. For instance, under my husband, Keith's, name I have written, "Your wisdom and direction." Since I am praying to God, "Your" obviously refers to God. My husband serves as husband, father, attorney, and deacon; God knows what I mean when Keith is in the midst of major decisions.

In my column, I may pray for "Your Patience," if I am going through a trying time. For a child I may pray, "Increase understanding," if a difficult subject is being studied. Or I may pray, "Desire You," if the world is vying for a person's attention.

One lady calls her family every Sunday and asks how she can pray for them for the following week. They now anticipate her call and look forward to sharing prayer requests with her.

The "Friends" column provides a place to record prayers for your friends. What a sweet privilege it is to pray for strength in marriages, guidance in raising children, help in meeting financial needs, patience in the home, and growth in the Lord.

The "Ministry" column is where you can record prayer requests related to your particular area of service or volunteer work. Your ministry may be teaching a Sunday school class, leading a Bible study, visiting nursing homes, encouraging those with whom you work, or ministering to your extended family.

The "Church" column is for pastors, leaders, and events going on within the church. It is here you can pray for God's direction, the Holy Spirit's anointing, for unity within the body, and outreach opportunities. A friend of mine calls her pastor each week and asks for specific ways she can pray for him.

You may want to take your prayer journal with you to your Sunday school class or Bible study and record prayer requests under a separate column heading. You can designate a whole column to your class's requests and pray for the class as you go through the week. When weekly praises are given, you can easily turn to the prior week and highlight or date answered prayer. Imagine the blessing to your friends as they realize you are taking their prayer requests before the throne of God each week!

The "Unsaved" and "USA" columns are places to record prayer requests for unsaved individuals and for the United States and her elected officials. Or you may choose to combine the two subjects into one column.

Additional columns allow you to have headings for other friends, ministry projects, coworkers, persons, or areas you are praying for. These column headings can change depending on the events in your life or projects with which you are involved.

Don't worry about grammar or punctuation. Use initials for names and abbreviation for words.

By recording prayer needs in a downward column, you can easily trace God's hand in the lives of those for whom you are praying. As with the "Month at a Glance" format, a check mark, date, or highlighting can record answered prayer. Writing PTL for "Praise the Lord!" blesses you, as well as others, when you share God's answers.

Meditations, Notes, and Prayers

In the final section of your journal, you will find pages with blank lines on which to record your thoughts, prayers, confessions, praises, ideas, and direction—whatever you receive while in prayer with God. Some of my most precious moments have been in stillness before the Father. With pen in hand, Bible and journal open, I find that God brings to mind poems, ministry direction, and ideas for what God would have me do. The joy of intimacy with the Savior is abundant!

In addition, sermon and personal Bible study notes can be recorded in this section. When you go before the Father with the notes you have taken, you can ask that He make the teachings real and applicable in your life or in the life of a loved one for whom you are praying. Bible study notes can be transforming when we ask the Father to change our hearts according to the Word He has given us.

Inspiration

Prayer journaling, for me, is inspirational! Why?

First of all, prayer is not just about us pouring out our requests to God, but also about God pouring His will into us—what He is doing and accomplishing.

Can you imagine the disciples "telling" Jesus where they were going next on their mission journey, how they were going to get there, and who they were going to heal? Instead, we find the disciples following Jesus and listening to His instructions. Yes, at times they questioned Him. "Rabbi, the Jews were just now seeking to stone You and are You going there again?" (John 11:8). But then they listened and followed.

Many times I have knelt with my Bible open and my prayer journal in hand, not knowing how to pray. But in those times of quietness and silence, the Lord has directed me how to pray even as Romans 8:26 says. In those times, the Holy Spirit brings to mind prayer requests with direction and insight that I would not have even thought of. The joy of being led by God's Spirit, recording His requests, is abundant!

In those moments prayer becomes dynamic and didactic! It becomes two-way communication with the Father. On the paper you see only words, but in lives you see change as the dynamic Spirit of God the Father moves on behalf of His children and kingdom.

A Tool in the Master's Hands

This prayer journal is simply a tool to help you accomplish God's will that you pray. Be careful not to be legalistic about journaling every day, or perhaps even every week, or to impose our appreciation of prayer journaling on others. On the other hand, we must not neglect the privilege of hearing God's direction and seeing His hand in our lives and others'.

Yes, this prayer journal is only a tool. But a tool in the Master's hands can bring forth fruit. I pray that as you make intentional time with God each day that you will discover the blessing of intimacy with Him, of seeing God answer your recorded petitions, of unexpected meditations flowing from your pen. Exultation to the Father, joy, and praise flow freely when one is *engaged* in communion with the living, eternal God! May I encourage you to enter into the joy of your Master as you commune with and serve Him through prayer!

As Jesus taught us to pray, may we pray.

As He modeled the importance of prayer by His early rising to pray, may we follow His example!

In Christ's Love,

Debbie

Examples of how to use "Month at a Glance," "Week at a Glance," and "Meditations, Notes, and Prayers" can be found in the appendix.

my prayer journal

The LORD is near to all who call upon Him,
To all who call upon Him in truth.—*Psalm 145:18*

month at a *glance*

prayer requests

month at a *glance*

"O LORD, I call upon You; hasten to me! Give ear to my voice when I call to You! May my prayer be counted as incense before You; the lifting up of my hands as the evening offering."—*Psalm 141:1–2*

sunday	monday	tuesday	wednesday	thursday	friday	saturday

month at a *glance*

"I love the LORD, because He hears my voice and my supplications."—*Psalm 116:1*

sunday	monday	tuesday	wednesday	thursday	friday	saturday

month at a *glance*

"In my trouble I cried to the LORD, and He answered me."—*Psalm 120:1*

sunday	monday	tuesday	wednesday	thursday	friday	saturday

month at a *glance*

April_____

"I will say to the LORD, 'My refuge and my fortress, my God, in whom I trust!'"—*Psalm 91:2*

sunday	monday	tuesday	wednesday	thursday	friday	saturday

month at a *glance*

May_____

"The LORD hears the needy and does not despise His who are prisoners."—*Psalm 69:33*

sunday	monday	tuesday	wednesday	thursday	friday	saturday

month at a *glance*

June_____

sunday	monday	tuesday	wednesday	thursday	friday	saturday

month at a *glance*

July_____

"Wash me thoroughly from my iniquity and cleanse me from my sin.
For I know my transgressions, and my sin is ever before me."—*Psalm 51:2–3*

sunday	monday	tuesday	wednesday	thursday	friday	saturday

month at a *glance*

"My soul waits for the Lord more than the watchmen for the morning;
Indeed, more than the watchmen for the morning."—*Psalm 130:6*

sunday	monday	tuesday	wednesday	thursday	friday	saturday

month at a *glance*

"In my distress I called upon the LORD, and cried to my God for help; He heard my voice out of His temple, And my cry for help before Him came into His ears."—*Psalm 18:6*

sunday	monday	tuesday	wednesday	thursday	friday	saturday

month at a *glance*

October_____

"If I regard wickedness in my heart, the Lord will not hear; but certainly God has heard;
He has given heed to the voice of my prayer."—*Psalm 66:18–19*

sunday	monday	tuesday	wednesday	thursday	friday	saturday

month at a *glance*

"The Everlasting God, the LORD, the creator of the ends of the earth does not become weary or tired.
His understanding is inscrutable."—*Isaiah 40:2–3*

sunday	monday	tuesday	wednesday	thursday	friday	saturday

month at a *glance*

"Every day I will bless You, and I will praise Your name forever and ever."—*Psalm 145:2*

sunday	monday	tuesday	wednesday	thursday	friday	saturday

week at a *glance*

prayer requests

week at a *glance*

prayers for my family

sunday					
monday					
tuesday					
wednesday					
thursday					
friday					
saturday					

"I say to you, ask, and it will be given to you; seek, and you will find;
knock, and it will be opened to you."—*Luke 11:9*

week of_____

prayers for others

sunday						
monday						
tuesday						
wednesday						
thursday						
friday						
saturday						

week at a *glance*

prayers for my family

sunday					
monday					
tuesday					
wednesday					
thursday					
friday					
saturday					

"Whatever you ask in My name, that will I do, so that the Father may be glorified in the Son."—*John 14:13*

week of_____

prayers for others

sunday					
monday					
tuesday					
wednesday					
thursday					
friday					
saturday					

week at a *glance*

prayers for my family

sunday						
monday						
tuesday						
wednesday						
thursday						
friday						
saturday						

"It will also come to pass that before they call, I will answer; and while they are still speaking, I will hear."—Isaiah 65:24

week of_____

prayers for others

sunday					
monday					
tuesday					
wednesday					
thursday					
friday					
saturday					

week at a *glance*

prayers for my family

sunday					
monday					
tuesday					
wednesday					
thursday					
friday					
saturday					

"Call to Me and I will answer you, and I will tell you great and mighty things, which you do not know."—*Jeremiah 33:3*

week of_____

prayers for others

sunday						
monday						
tuesday						
wednesday						
thursday						
friday						
saturday						

week at a *glance*

prayers for my family

sunday					
monday					
tuesday					
wednesday					
thursday					
friday					
saturday					

"If you abide in Me, and My words abide in you, ask whatever you wish, and it will be done for you."—*John 15:7*

week of_____

prayers for others

sunday						
monday						
tuesday						
wednesday						
thursday						
friday						
saturday						

week at a *glance*

prayers for my family

sunday					
monday					
tuesday					
wednesday					
thursday					
friday					
saturday					

"And whatever we ask we receive from Him, because we keep His commandments and do the things that are pleasing in His sight."—*1 John 3:22*

week of_____

prayers for others

sunday						
monday						
tuesday						
wednesday						
thursday						
friday						
saturday						

week at a *glance*

prayers for my family

sunday					
monday					
tuesday					
wednesday					
thursday					
friday					
saturday					

"Confess your sins to one another, and pray for one another so that you may be healed."—*James 5:16*

week of_____

prayers for others

sunday					
monday					
tuesday					
wednesday					
thursday					
friday					
saturday					

week at a *glance*

prayers for my family

sunday					
monday					
tuesday					
wednesday					
thursday					
friday					
saturday					

"You will seek Me and find Me when you search for Me with all your heart."—Jeremiah 29:13

week of_____

prayers for others

sunday					
monday					
tuesday					
wednesday					
thursday					
friday					
saturday					

week at a *glance*

prayers for my family

sunday						
monday						
tuesday						
wednesday						
thursday						
friday						
saturday						

"If . . . My people who are called by My name humble themselves and pray and seek My face and turn from their wicked ways, then I will hear from heaven, will forgive their sin and will heal their land."—*2 Chronicles 7:13–14*

week of_____

prayers for others

sunday						
monday						
tuesday						
wednesday						
thursday						
friday						
saturday						

week at a *glance*

prayers for my family

sunday						
monday						
tuesday						
wednesday						
thursday						
friday						
saturday						

"This is the confidence which we have before Him, that, if we ask anything according to His will, He hears us. And if we know that He hears us in whatever we ask, we know that we have the requests which we have asked from Him."—*1 John 5:14–15*

week of_____

prayers for others

sunday						
monday						
tuesday						
wednesday						
thursday						
friday						
saturday						

week at a *glance*

prayers for my family

sunday						
monday						
tuesday						
wednesday						
thursday						
friday						
saturday						

"The righteous cry, and the LORD hears and delivers them out of all their troubles."—*Psalm 34:17*

week of_____

prayers for others

sunday					
monday					
tuesday					
wednesday					
thursday					
friday					
saturday					

week at a *glance*

prayers for my family

sunday					
monday					
tuesday					
wednesday					
thursday					
friday					
saturday					

"On God my salvation and my glory rest; the rock of my strength, my refuge is in God."—Psalm 62:7

week of_____

prayers for others

sunday						
monday						
tuesday						
wednesday						
thursday						
friday						
saturday						

week at a *glance*

prayers for my family

sunday					
monday					
tuesday					
wednesday					
thursday					
friday					
saturday					

"The LORD is far from the wicked, but He hears the prayer of the righteous."—*Proverbs 15:29*

week of_____

prayers for others

sunday					
monday					
tuesday					
wednesday					
thursday					
friday					
saturday					

week at a *glance*

prayers for my family

sunday						
monday						
tuesday						
wednesday						
thursday						
friday						
saturday						

"But as for me, I will watch expectantly for the LORD; I will wait for the God of my salvation."—Micah 7:7

week of_____

prayers for others

sunday					
monday					
tuesday					
wednesday					
thursday					
friday					
saturday					

week at a *glance*

prayers for my family

sunday					
monday					
tuesday					
wednesday					
thursday					
friday					
saturday					

"In the same way the Spirit also helps our weakness; for we do not know how to pray as we should, but the Spirit Himself intercedes for us with groanings too deep for words."—*Romans 8:26*

week of_____

prayers for others

sunday					
monday					
tuesday					
wednesday					
thursday					
friday					
saturday					

week at a *glance*

prayers for my family

sunday					
monday					
tuesday					
wednesday					
thursday					
friday					
saturday					

"When you are praying, do not use meaningless repetition as the Gentiles do, for they suppose that they will be heard for their many words."—*Matthew 6:7*

week of_____

prayers for others

sunday						
monday						
tuesday						
wednesday						
thursday						
friday						
saturday						

week at a *glance*

prayers for my family

sunday					
monday					
tuesday					
wednesday					
thursday					
friday					
saturday					

"In God I have put my trust, I shall not be afraid. What can man do to me?"—*Psalm 56:11*

week of_____

prayers for others

sunday					
monday					
tuesday					
wednesday					
thursday					
friday					
saturday					

week at a *glance*

prayers for my family

sunday						
monday						
tuesday						
wednesday						
thursday						
friday						
saturday						

"Let us draw near with confidence to the throne of grace,
so that we may receive mercy and find grace to help in time of need."—*Hebrews 4:16*

week of_____

prayers for others

sunday					
monday					
tuesday					
wednesday					
thursday					
friday					
saturday					

week at a *glance*

prayers for my family

sunday					
monday					
tuesday					
wednesday					
thursday					
friday					
saturday					

week of_____

prayers for others

sunday					
monday					
tuesday					
wednesday					
thursday					
friday					
saturday					

week at a *glance*

prayers for my family

sunday					
monday					
tuesday					
wednesday					
thursday					
friday					
saturday					

"But you, when you pray, go into your inner room, close your door and pray to your Father who is in secret, and your Father who sees what is done in secret will reward you."—*Matthew 6:6*

week of_____

prayers for others

sunday						
monday						
tuesday						
wednesday						
thursday						
friday						
saturday						

week at a *glance*

prayers for my family

sunday					
monday					
tuesday					
wednesday					
thursday					
friday					
saturday					

"Until now you have asked for nothing in My name;
ask and you will receive, so that your joy may be made full."—*John 16:24*

prayers for others

sunday					
monday					
tuesday					
wednesday					
thursday					
friday					
saturday					

week at a *glance*

prayers for my family

sunday					
monday					
tuesday					
wednesday					
thursday					
friday					
saturday					

"My God will supply all your needs according to His riches in glory in Christ Jesus."—*Philippians 4:19*

week of_____

prayers for others

sunday					
monday					
tuesday					
wednesday					
thursday					
friday					
saturday					

week at a *glance*

prayers for my family

sunday					
monday					
tuesday					
wednesday					
thursday					
friday					
saturday					

"All things you ask in prayer, believing, you will receive."—Matthew 21:22

week of_____

prayers for others

sunday					
monday					
tuesday					
wednesday					
thursday					
friday					
saturday					

week at a *glance*

prayers for my family

sunday						
monday						
tuesday						
wednesday						
thursday						
friday						
saturday						

"Again I say to you, that if two of you agree on earth about anything that they may ask, it shall be done for them by My Father who is in heaven."—Matthew 18:19

week of_____

prayers for others

sunday					
monday					
tuesday					
wednesday					
thursday					
friday					
saturday					

week at a *glance*

prayers for my family

sunday						
monday						
tuesday						
wednesday						
thursday						
friday						
saturday						

"With all prayer and petition pray at all times in the Spirit, and with this in view,
be on the alert with all perseverance and petition for all the saints."—*Ephesians 6:18*

week of_____

prayers for others

sunday						
monday						
tuesday						
wednesday						
thursday						
friday						
saturday						

week at a *glance*

prayers for my family

sunday					
monday					
tuesday					
wednesday					
thursday					
friday					
saturday					

"Devote yourselves to prayer, keeping alert in it with an attitude of thanksgiving."—*Colossians 4:2*

week of_____

prayers for others

sunday					
monday					
tuesday					
wednesday					
thursday					
friday					
saturday					

week at a *glance*

prayers for my family

sunday						
monday						
tuesday						
wednesday						
thursday						
friday						
saturday						

"I want the men in every place to pray, lifting up holy hands,
without wrath and dissension."—*1 Timothy 2:8*

week of_____

prayers for others

sunday					
monday					
tuesday					
wednesday					
thursday					
friday					
saturday					

week at a *glance*

prayers for my family

sunday					
monday					
tuesday					
wednesday					
thursday					
friday					
saturday					

"Lead me in Your truth and teach me, for You are the God of my salvation;
for You I will wait all the day."—*Psalm 25:5*

week of_____

prayers for others

sunday					
monday					
tuesday					
wednesday					
thursday					
friday					
saturday					

week at a *glance*

prayers for my family

sunday					
monday					
tuesday					
wednesday					
thursday					
friday					
saturday					

"The effective prayer of a righteous man can accomplish much."—James 5:16

week of_____

prayers for others

sunday					
monday					
tuesday					
wednesday					
thursday					
friday					
saturday					

week at a *glance*

prayers for my family

sunday					
monday					
tuesday					
wednesday					
thursday					
friday					
saturday					

"Those who know Your name will put their trust in You,
For You, O LORD, have not forsaken those who seek you."—*Psalm 9:10*

week of_____

prayers for others

sunday						
monday						
tuesday						
wednesday						
thursday						
friday						
saturday						

week at a *glance*

prayers for my family

sunday					
monday					
tuesday					
wednesday					
thursday					
friday					
saturday					

"Answer me when I call, O God of my righteousness!
You have relieved me in my distress; be gracious to me and hear my prayer."—*Psalm 4:1*

week of_____

prayers for others

sunday						
monday						
tuesday						
wednesday						
thursday						
friday						
saturday						

week at a *glance*

prayers for my family

sunday					
monday					
tuesday					
wednesday					
thursday					
friday					
saturday					

"Give ear to my words, O LORD, consider my groaning. Heed the sound of my cry for help, my King and my God, for to You I pray."—*Psalm 5:1–2*

week of_____

prayers for others

sunday					
monday					
tuesday					
wednesday					
thursday					
friday					
saturday					

week at a *glance*

prayers for my family

sunday					
monday					
tuesday					
wednesday					
thursday					
friday					
saturday					

"In the morning, O LORD, You will hear my voice;
In the morning I will order my prayer to You and eagerly watch."—*Psalm 5:3*

week of_____

prayers for others

sunday					
monday					
tuesday					
wednesday					
thursday					
friday					
saturday					

week at a *glance*

prayers for my family

sunday					
monday					
tuesday					
wednesday					
thursday					
friday					
saturday					

"O LORD, the God of my salvation, I have cried out by day and in the night before You.
Let my prayer come before You; incline Your ear to my cry!"—*Psalm 88:1–2*

week of_____

prayers for others

sunday						
monday						
tuesday						
wednesday						
thursday						
friday						
saturday						

week at a *glance*

prayers for my family

sunday					
monday					
tuesday					
wednesday					
thursday					
friday					
saturday					

"God is our refuge and our strength, a very present help in trouble. Therefore we will not fear, though the earth should change and though the mountains slip into the heart of the sea."—*Psalm 46:1–2*

week of_____

prayers for others

sunday					
monday					
tuesday					
wednesday					
thursday					
friday					
saturday					

week at a *glance*

prayers for my family

sunday					
monday					
tuesday					
wednesday					
thursday					
friday					
saturday					

"O Lord my God, I cried to You for help, and You healed me."—Psalm 30:2

week of_____

prayers for others

sunday						
monday						
tuesday						
wednesday						
thursday						
friday						
saturday						

week at a *glance*

prayers for my family

sunday					
monday					
tuesday					
wednesday					
thursday					
friday					
saturday					

"O God, You are my God; I shall seek You earnestly; my soul thirsts for You,
my flesh yearns for You, in a dry and weary land where there is no water."—*Psalm 63:1*

week of_____

prayers for others

sunday					
monday					
tuesday					
wednesday					
thursday					
friday					
saturday					

week at a *glance*

prayers for my family

sunday					
monday					
tuesday					
wednesday					
thursday					
friday					
saturday					

"Our help is in the name of the LORD, who made heaven and earth."—*Psalm 124:8*

week of_____

prayers for others

sunday						
monday						
tuesday						
wednesday						
thursday						
friday						
saturday						

week at a *glance*

prayers for my family

sunday					
monday					
tuesday					
wednesday					
thursday					
friday					
saturday					

"My soul waits in silence for God only; from Him is my salvation."—Psalm 62:1

week of_____

prayers for others

sunday					
monday					
tuesday					
wednesday					
thursday					
friday					
saturday					

week at a *glance*

prayers for my family

sunday						
monday						
tuesday						
wednesday						
thursday						
friday						
saturday						

"Seek the LORD and His strength; seek His face continually. Remember His wonders which He has done, His marvels and the judgments uttered by His mouth."—*Psalm 105:4–5*

week of_____

prayers for others

sunday						
monday						
tuesday						
wednesday						
thursday						
friday						
saturday						

week at a *glance*

prayers for my family

sunday					
monday					
tuesday					
wednesday					
thursday					
friday					
saturday					

"Hear my voice according to Your lovingkindness; revive me, O LORD,
according to Your ordinances."—*Psalm 119:149*

week of_____

prayers for others

sunday						
monday						
tuesday						
wednesday						
thursday						
friday						
saturday						

week at a *glance*

prayers for my family

sunday					
monday					
tuesday					
wednesday					
thursday					
friday					
saturday					

"Evening and morning and at noon, I will complain and murmur, and He will hear my voice. He will redeem my soul in peace from the battle which is against me, for they are many who strive with me."—Psalm 55:17–18

week of_____

prayers for others

sunday					
monday					
tuesday					
wednesday					
thursday					
friday					
saturday					

week at a *glance*

prayers for my family

sunday					
monday					
tuesday					
wednesday					
thursday					
friday					
saturday					

"God will hear and answer them—even the one who sits enthroned from of old."—*Psalm 55:19*

week of_____

prayers for others

sunday					
monday					
tuesday					
wednesday					
thursday					
friday					
saturday					

week at a *glance*

prayers for my family

sunday					
monday					
tuesday					
wednesday					
thursday					
friday					
saturday					

"Cast your burden upon the LORD and He will sustain you;
He will never allow the righteous to be shaken."—*Psalm 55:22*

week of_____

prayers for others

sunday						
monday						
tuesday						
wednesday						
thursday						
friday						
saturday						

week at a *glance*

prayers for my family

sunday					
monday					
tuesday					
wednesday					
thursday					
friday					
saturday					

"You have taken account of my wanderings; put my tears in Your bottle. Are they not in Your book?"—*Psalm 56:8*

week of_____

prayers for others

sunday					
monday					
tuesday					
wednesday					
thursday					
friday					
saturday					

week at a *glance*

prayers for my family

sunday						
monday						
tuesday						
wednesday						
thursday						
friday						
saturday						

"For You have delivered my soul from death, indeed my feet from stumbling,
So that I may walk before God in the light of the living."—*Psalm 56:13*

week of_____

prayers for others

sunday						
monday						
tuesday						
wednesday						
thursday						
friday						
saturday						

week at a *glance*

prayers for my family

sunday					
monday					
tuesday					
wednesday					
thursday					
friday					
saturday					

"Be gracious to me, O God, be gracious to me, for my soul takes refuge in You;
And in the shadow of Your wings I will take refuge until destruction passes by."—*Psalm 57:1*

week of_____

prayers for others

sunday					
monday					
tuesday					
wednesday					
thursday					
friday					
saturday					

week at a *glance*

prayers for my family

sunday					
monday					
tuesday					
wednesday					
thursday					
friday					
saturday					

"Give ear to my prayer, O God; and do not hide Yourself from my supplication."—*Psalm 55:1*

week of_____

prayers for others

sunday						
monday						
tuesday						
wednesday						
thursday						
friday						
saturday						

week at a *glance*

prayers for my family

sunday						
monday						
tuesday						
wednesday						
thursday						
friday						
saturday						

"The LORD will command His lovingkindness in the daytime; and His song will be with me in the night,
A prayer to the God of my life."—*Psalm 42:8*

week of_____

prayers for others

sunday					
monday					
tuesday					
wednesday					
thursday					
friday					
saturday					

week at a *glance*

prayers for my family

sunday					
monday					
tuesday					
wednesday					
thursday					
friday					
saturday					

"Why are you in despair, O my soul? And why are you disturbed within me? Hope in God, for I shall again praise Him, the help of my countenance and my God."—*Psalm 43:5*

week of_____

prayers for others

sunday					
monday					
tuesday					
wednesday					
thursday					
friday					
saturday					

week at a *glance*

prayers for my family

sunday					
monday					
tuesday					
wednesday					
thursday					
friday					
saturday					

"O clap your hands, all peoples; shout to God with the voice of joy.
For the LORD Most High is to be feared, a great King over all the earth."—*Psalm 47:1–2*

week of_____

prayers for others

sunday					
monday					
tuesday					
wednesday					
thursday					
friday					
saturday					

week at a *glance*

prayers for my family

sunday						
monday						
tuesday						
wednesday						
thursday						
friday						
saturday						

"Be anxious for nothing, but in everything by prayer and supplication with thanksgiving
let your requests be made known to God. And the peace of God, which surpasses all comprehension,
will guard your hearts and your minds in Christ Jesus."—*Philippians 4:6–7*

week of_____

prayers for others

sunday						
monday						
tuesday						
wednesday						
thursday						
friday						
saturday						

meditations, notes, and prayers

meditations, notes, and prayers

"Great is the LORD, and highly to be praised; and His greatness is unsearchable." —Psalm 145:3

meditations, notes, and prayers

"The LORD is gracious and merciful; slow to anger and great in lovingkindness." —Psalm 145:8

meditations, notes, and prayers

"The LORD is good to all, and His mercies are over all His works." —Psalm 145:9

meditations, notes, and prayers

"Be strong and let your heart take courage, all you who hope in the LORD." —Psalm 31:24

meditations, notes, and prayers

"As is Your name, O God, so is Your praise to the ends of the earth;
Your right hand is full of righteousness." —Psalm 48:10

meditations, notes, and prayers

_____

_____

_____

_____

_____

_____

_____

_____

_____

_____

_____

_____

_____

_____

_____

_____

_____

_____

_____

_____

_____

_____

_____

_____

_____

"The LORD preserves the simple; I was brought low, and He saved me." —Psalm 116:6

meditations, notes, and prayers

meditations, notes, and prayers

"Gracious is the LORD, and righteous; yes, our God is compassionate." —Psalm 116:5

meditations, notes, and prayers

"Return to your rest, O my soul, for the LORD has dealt bountifully with you." —Psalm 116:7

meditations, notes, and prayers

_____

_____

_____

_____

_____

_____

_____

_____

_____

_____

_____

_____

_____

_____

_____

_____

_____

_____

_____

_____

_____

_____

"I shall lift up the cup of salvation and call upon the name of the LORD." —Psalm 116:13

meditations, notes, and prayers

_____

_____

_____

_____

_____

_____

_____

_____

_____

_____

_____

_____

_____

_____

_____

_____

_____

_____

_____

_____

_____

_____

"Hear my cry, O God; give heed to my prayer." —Psalm 61:1

meditations, notes, and prayers

"He who dwells in the shelter of the Most High
Will abide in the shadow of the Almighty." —Psalm 91:1

meditations, notes, and prayers

"To You I lift up my eyes, O You who are enthroned in the heavens!" —Psalm 123:1

meditations, notes, and prayers

"Because Your lovingkindness is better than life, my lips will praise You." —Psalm 63:3

meditations, notes, and prayers

_____

_____

_____

_____

_____

_____

_____

_____

_____

_____

_____

_____

_____

_____

_____

_____

_____

_____

_____

_____

"The LORD has done great things for us; we are glad." —Psalm 126:3

meditations, notes, and prayers

"Those who sow in tears shall reap with joyful shouting." —Psalm 126:5

meditations, notes, and prayers

"The grass withers, the flower fades, but the word of our God stands forever." —Isaiah 40:8

meditations, notes, and prayers

_____

_____

_____

_____

_____

_____

_____

_____

_____

_____

_____

_____

_____

_____

_____

_____

_____

_____

_____

_____

_____

_____

_____

"When I remember You on my bed, I meditate on You in the night watches." —Psalm 63:6

meditations, notes, and prayers

"For You have been my help, and in the shadow of Your wings I sing for joy." —Psalm 63:7

meditations, notes, and prayers

"My soul clings to You; Your right hand upholds me." —Psalm 63:8

meditations, notes, and prayers

"I will bless You as long as I live; I will lift up my hands in Your name." —Psalm 63:4

meditations, notes, and prayers

"My soul, wait in silence for God only, for my hope is from Him." —Psalm 62:5

meditations, notes, and prayers

"He only is my rock and my salvation, My stronghold; I shall not be shaken." —Psalm 62:6

meditations, notes, and prayers

_____

_____

_____

_____

_____

_____

_____

_____

_____

_____

_____

_____

_____

_____

_____

_____

_____

_____

_____

_____

"Let my meditation be pleasing to Him;
As for me, I shall be glad in the LORD." —Psalm 104:34

meditations, notes, and prayers

_____
_____
_____
_____
_____
_____
_____
_____
_____
_____
_____
_____
_____
_____
_____
_____
_____
_____
_____

"Hear, O LORD, and be gracious to me; O LORD, be my helper." —Psalm 30:10

meditations, notes, and prayers

_____
_____
_____
_____
_____
_____
_____
_____
_____
_____
_____
_____
_____
_____
_____
_____
_____
_____
_____
_____
_____

"I cried to You; save me and I shall keep Your testimonies." —Psalm 119:146

meditations, notes, and prayers

"I rise before dawn and cry for help; I wait for Your words." —Psalm 119:147

meditations, notes, and prayers

_____

_____

_____

_____

_____

_____

_____

_____

_____

_____

_____

_____

_____

_____

_____

_____

_____

_____

_____

_____

_____

"My eyes anticipate the night watches, that I may meditate on Your word." —Psalm 119:148

meditations, notes, and prayers

"You are near, O LORD, and all Your commandments are truth." —Psalm 119:151

meditations, notes, and prayers

"Give thanks to the LORD, for He is good; for His lovingkindness is everlasting." —Psalm 118:29

meditations, notes, and prayers

"O God, hasten to deliver me; O LORD, hasten to my help!" —Psalm 70:1

meditations, notes, and prayers

_____

_____

_____

_____

_____

_____

_____

_____

_____

_____

_____

_____

_____

_____

_____

_____

_____

_____

_____

_____

"Look upon my affliction and rescue me, for I do not forget Your law." —Psalm 119:153

appendix

month at a *glance (Sample)*

Month/Year

"O LORD, I call upon You; hasten to me! Give ear to my voice when I call to You! May my prayer be counted as incense before You; the lifting up of my hands as the evening offering."—*Psalm 141:1–2*

sunday	monday	tuesday	wednesday	thursday	friday	saturday
					John & Mary—trial	
		John—surgery **PTL**			*Women's Retreat—safe and joyful arrival. God's anointing on speakers, music.*	*Retreat—God's blessing on all. Changed lives.* **PTL**
Sara—attend with me. **PTL**				*Linda—birthday*		
	Bob—funeral					*Peter & Liz— traveling safety* **PTL**
			Amber—test			

* PTL = Praise the Lord!

week at a *glance (Sample)*   week of_____

prayers for my family

	Keith	Debbie	Taylor	Lauren	Family	Friends
sunday	Your wisdom & direction **PTL**	Fill with Your Holy Spirit. Reflect Your love today	Direct which college to go to	Grow in knowledge of You **PTL**	Mom—quick recovery from surgery	Sam & Paula—reconcile
monday	Use as light at work **PTL**	Your patience/peace	Read & love your word **PTL**		Bro—find church home **PTL**	Lou—help overcome hurt
tuesday	Use us to minister to Sarah & Bill		Hunger for You **PTL**	Desire You	Uncle—turn heart to You. J & P—strengthen marriage.	Karen—Dr's wisdom. Mark—find You sufficient in all things.
wednesday	Strength to meet demands	Your words to speak	Give energy to meet demands	Increase understanding	Carol—discipline and self-control. Jack—draw to Your Word.	Mindy—open door to new job if Your will
thursday						
friday						
saturday						

"You have taken account of my wanderings;
put my tears in Your bottle. Are they not in Your book?"—*Psalm 56:8*

week of_____

prayers for others

	Ministry	Church	Bible Study	Unsaved	USA	Others
sunday	Seekers attend PTL	Pastor—equipped. Inspired to preach in power of Holy Spirit.	Carol—business used for Your glory	Sue—convince of need for You	Guide president	Larry's parents—open hearts to You PTL
monday	Christians grow in knowledge of You	Leaders—wisdom PTL	Jackie—surgery successful PTL	Ty—desire You	Elections	Bill—Jack be good steward of money
tuesday	Use to spread Your Word & love PTL	Passion for the unsaved	Mike—increased sensitivity to Your Spirit	Jo—read John	Turn hearts to You PTL	Betty—successful rehab. Make Your presence known to her.
wednesday	Equip leaders	Unity	Pat—patience at home, model your love	Pat—close doors to deceptive habits	Christians be lights and examples	
thursday						
friday						
saturday						

meditations, notes, and prayers *(sample)*

4/18/—Sunday morning sermon note: Faith is a reach muscle.

Lord, help me exercise my faith as I do my body. Strengthen me and build my faith so that I may serve You with greater energy and zeal. May I not shirk back from exercising faith in the challenges You put before me. May my faith become stronger so that I can serve You more fully through the empowerment of Your Spirit. Help my children practice their faith and not be soft or weak, but prepared and ready for the next challenge You put before them. Build them up to serve Your body, to Your glory, Lord. I love You and thank You.

_____

_____

_____

_____

_____

_____

_____

"As the deer pants for the water brooks, so my soul pants for You, O God." —Psalm 42:1

Hill Country Ministries, Inc.

is located in the beautiful hill country of Kerrville, Texas, forty-five miles northwest of San Antonio. Founded in 1999 as a 501C(3), its mission is to spread the Word and love of God. It serves both individuals and the church by providing Bible study resources and inspirational gifts for all ages—for both Bible students and seekers. Its goal is to reach those who do not know Christ with the knowledge of Him and to disciple the Christian in the grace and knowledge of the Lord Jesus Christ.

Debbie Taylor Williams

is founder and president of Hill Country Ministries. She has been teaching the Bible for more than twenty-five years and is the author of numerous Bible studies, including *Discovering His Passion; On Enemy Ground; A Glimpse of Jesus' Glory; Living by the Divine Nature; Knowing God in Psalms 1–20;* and *If God Is in Control, Why Do I Have a Headache?* Prior to leading a large community Bible study at her church, Debbie served as teaching leader for Bible Study Fellowship. She and her husband, Keith, have two children, Taylor and Lauren. Debbie speaks at conferences and events around the country and is known for her passion for Christ and ability to communicate and apply Scripture to everyday life. To schedule Debbie for a speaking engagement, contact Hill Country Ministries, Inc., at 830-257-5995, or e-mail her at hcm@ktc.com.

Friends of Hill Country Ministries

are those who support Hill Country Ministries by their prayers, volunteer support, and/or financial gifts. To find out how you can be a part of the ongoing work of Hill Country Ministries, please contact us at 830-257-5995, e-mail us at hcm@ktc.com, visit our Web site at http://www.hillcountryministries.org, or write to us at PO Box 2218, Kerrville, TX 78029-2218.

Bible Studies

- A Glimpse of Jesus' Glory—Luke
- Consider It All Joy—James
- Contend Earnestly for the Faith—Jude
- Discovering His Passion
- Focus through the Bible
- Grace and Peace in Fullest Measure—1 Peter
- How to Live by the Divine Nature—2 Peter
- If God Is in Control, Why Do I Have a Headache?
- In Touch with God, Volumes One and Two
- Jesus' Letters to the Churches—Revelation 1–3
- Knowing God in Psalms 1–20
- On Enemy Ground, On Holy Ground
- Wisdom With Thee Word

Inspirational Resources

- Cross Upon the Rock Paper Weight
- From My Heart Collection of Poetry
- Kid's Time Devotional Photo Journal
- Preparing Our Hearts for Christmas
- Rub-A-Dub-Dub Bible Poems for Tub

Workshops & Conferences

- A Leader's Heart Workshop
- Prayer Journaling Workshop/Conference Retreat
- Kid's Time Workshop
- Women of Passion & Purpose Annual Conference